WAITING FOR THE DAWN

BY

RICHARD NICHOLAS

THE SENTIENT PRESS

WAITING FOR THE DAWN

BY

RICHARD NICHOLAS

Maidstone
Printed by the University of Essex
1994

First Published in 1994
by The Sentient Press

British Library Cataloguing in Publication Data
Nicholas, Richard 1974-
Waiting for the Dawn.
1. Poetry.
1. Title.
ISBN-0-9521-270-1-6.

Published by The Sentient Press
A Division of D & P Communications
12, Grange House
Fernhill Road
Maidstone
Kent

The Sentient Press, set up in 1992, aims to publish writing of authorial quality and integrity.
It stresses the verisimilitude and magnificence of the written word, standing as a bastion for those yet published, yet heard.

Contents

Poetry

Prose

For Sophie

and my parents

for their endurance

Nightfall

The dragging scroach of high-heeled footsteps
Take an eternity
To reveal themselves;
Quickly draw away to leave a glow.
Rippled voices spread thinly outwards,
Lost in the tired yawl of streetlights,
Tediously keeping the empty stage alight,
The show, long over.

Engines start up and grumble away their sorrows.
Draining the dregs of red wine.
With a chill the night air throws shadows for scraps,
Pulls across its long cloak of silence.
The streetlight burrs its backstage sound,
Its final focus is sovereign.

Too tired for company

The cafe lights
Will carry the chink
Of words which shatter on the edge of a glass.
Your voice is unheard
But many are not
And heavy-peopled air won't weary the glow;
The night will slide
From the aching candle,
And coffee lies cold at the base of your cup.

<u>Impatient</u>

The young boy tugs at his mother's skirt
But it is no good-
She is too far away;
In heavy conversation with
Some other careless woman.
Each sighed word seems to mark the end
            ...Can we go?
A chance to ease the heaviness of his feet;
First one then the other he stands on.
Leaning out on outstretched arm
Makes not the slightest difference:
She is determined to ignore him,
But how can **she** know-
That in her easy greeting
To him whole hours of emotion are turning
And the sun is slinking low behind the trees.

Nightwatch

Across the night-heavy bay
With its shallow, swallowing currents
The swinging creak of a boat's rowing haunts
And murmuring of voices.
Echoing times, ages before
When smugglers gathered to welcome the plash;
The distancing, timeless plash of the oars
Groaning wood into swifting motion.
Tiny against the vast;
Overreaching, underspreading sky and sea
        Yet Persistent
        Echoing into the dust..

Breaking Oranges

After all the thick denial
Of powder-heavy, sour rind
Pulled away; a touch
Will break..and swollen segments
Taste opium, vivid as colour until:
The sticky, glinting juice
Runs sweet,
Too thick from punctured membrane;
Will suffocate to the root of your tongue,
Gills are gasping for air and guilt,
Too late! It holds no further and
Your hands are stained with
Orange cold.

Creature Comfort

Across the heavy,
Heathen cliff,
Where tangled branches claw
And stoke
Their vivid fires:
Fruit, for those so bold
To shelter from the gutsy gale
And hollow down, behind the flint,
Of aching sky, soaked blood-red,
The crown of thorns is tattered and
The eagle knows its prey.

An Encounter

The peacock, startled, stops.
Head cocked sideways it eyes me;
Questioning.
Have I the reverence to see through its eyes?
The wisdom to enter its peace?
In headlight-shock I'm searched,
Examined by the creature.
It seeks..has the time yet come?
And together we wait for my answer
But,
    Unsatisfied it drops,
    Not finding the knowledge in this stranger.
    We turn and regain our worlds.

Perpetuity

In quivering stillness the gull tapers off,
Tilting the sunrise, to slide
Around the side of a fading emotion,
Breaking off...
            To..
      ...Scree above the dappled water,
Wheeling under its reach.
Spinning the world with its eye
Unbounded, across an empty sea.
With nowhere to hide it can see the future,
Unaltered by time or space
Unfettered by evil it flows by its god.

Shifting mist clouds pelt inglorious rain
Yet it knows all there is,
As it drops down through space,
      And lands to shatter,
            The reflection of itself.

Sheep

The bruised clouds plunge
Their weight of water
Over cragged mist-space
Of unrelenting green;
Bearing no comfort for the sheep,
That shift uneasily on sodden ground
No one warned them of the cold up here,
The way the wind whips,
Bitter, through soaking hair
No question why? But now,
And the shivering
Waiting the eternity,
Whilst this different wind extracts its pain,
And the tugging of grass
Is loud when teeth rip.

Bloodthirst

As car-parks drain themselves, slowly of cars
And the sap of evening runs dry,
Traffic groans to itself about nothing
And grey clouds roll on the breeze.

Streetlight-pools nudge the final steps home
Like an arm outstretched to a drunkard.
A fluster of birds falls out of the trees
And spirals around to the rooftops.

Pavement-puddles sheen, upturned
The broken-ribbed glow of roadsigns
But as car doors slam and lounges fill up,
Outside the night shrugs off fear.

A cat bound the street, daring shadows unfolded,
Rolls a taste for blood on its tongue.
The eye-flick excitement streaking through fur.
Its kingdom has only begun...

Early Bird

(Sunset over the farm)

From the roof-shadow leaning
Across furrowed fields,
Flies an un-hurried owl
From his homely gable.
The shutters are open in spite of the sun-
Not the time for an owl,
But shelter's not far,
An aching reach...
      Across fields overspilled
         By sunlight, dragging
            Unwilling time behind it.

It is a cool perch
And easy to wait for
The darkness flood.

The View

(Day dreaming)

Through the market town
The river herds its flood.
Wanderers move
   Over the fields,
      Out of the town,
Away from the clock-tower;
Weighing instead the rhythm of the current
Into a clearer no-time,
Of the sun:

"Will they follow its tug,
To an easy death in the sea,
Till it breaks out its ripples at the shore
And imagine that the world has ended?..."

Clacton Winter

Balancing on the harbour wall
The pier is closed for winter;
Eccentric rainbow beach huts crowd:
Hugged up against the cold.

Here on tattered shore of the island
Where gusts blow sea-birds off-course
Kites are being flown and stones;
Skimmed over flinted sea.
The winter habitants have returned,

Soon as algie, when left unattended.
Yet this is the truth, behind the facade
Where land meets open sea;
The salted rope-burn on fisherman's palm,
Chips in an English, drizzled out bar.
And a few odd shapes walk tall
On the crumbling harbour wall,
Skimming stones at the plunging horizon.

Trees

From the very soul of the earth
Wrenched up,
Primitive secrets though a core of muscle

With strained sinews
A proud, tortured burden
Humbly carried

The knowledge of the dead
In mathematical perfection
Reaches upwards in prayer

1,1,2,3,5,8*
It builds
A spiritual guide for the wonder of the living

Lines of thought
Drawn out into branches
Where a mind may soar and perch.

Hushing the breeze
A comfort for those who must yet die alone
Like the dappled pattern of its shadow in the sun...
"Do not worry, there is reason
Time is gentle belonging"

*See Over

*1,1,2,3,5,8...etc. :A number sequence devised by Leopold Fibonacci in the 13th century, where each number is the sum of the two preceding numbers. In the 19th century scientists began to discover this sequence in nature, such as the arrangement of leaf buds on a stem, in the spirals of sunflower heads, in pine cones and...in the branching of trees.

Source: Encyclopaedia Britannica

No need to fear

Some nights we dream.
Some nights we do not dream
And never know why.
Sensations overwhelm and lead us through life.

Other times its black:

Not a fearful darkness, but an easy, gentle black
To which we submit with a shouldering roll.

If so what then?..

Shall we seep into the story
Of a further unfolding dream-scape
Or lie unwoken in a gentle peace?
Either way there is no need to fear;

There is nothing lacking.

Enjoy the day but,
Being over
There will be no further ending.
For only in this shallow time
Must love not last forever:
Once dear sleep unravels our minds
The ultimate knowledge will be ours, we

        Will not need to question
                                        Any more.

Bored with words

Bored with words I chide
And shield
My pages from unwoldiness,
To stop the frugal mattered
Spatt. Of tattered ends
And measured gobbles
Falling flat
On weakling shreds,
Morose-uncalm in their defence,
Unfriendly by their difference,
To each uneasy wave of sound,

I
Stop the page before it moves
And fold it up with a flurrr...

Spin Doctor

Just as we'd all become
Used to the sun,
Arching over the church
To sink,
Heavily, under the trees:
Galileo-the fool!
      Reached out...
            stopped it.
Cat-a-pulted the world around,
Spinning from shock,
Out in space.

Loveless

Orange glow:
As she draws her cigarette
It lights up her chin, her nose, her eyes
"So this is all?"
Is all she can think
Of the flesh-drowned comfort
She took tonight
No love,
No romance,
No easy trust to dream in
But only this;
The stark, real, certainty
That flees from death with a shiver:
The night is cold,
And they share nothing
But a sadness that lingers
In the words she didn't say.

Escapee

He jumped.

And when he kicked the ground he ran,
He ran until he felt the flood
(his lungs were frozen by the air)
The only sound was pounding blood,
And images hurt his teeming mind
But this was free,
This felt **good**
        -he grinned;

Almost as if it wasn't his body,
Lying smashed in a heap on the road.

Inevitable

And after the scream
A silence.
Nobody dared to move;
To turn and look at the truth
Was more than anyone could bear
And so we stood,
Suspended in time:
The headlight-shock held us together,
But still the moment tumbled in space;

And we knew.

Paralysed

Somewhere else high-heeled shoes
Hit the pavement with a clatter;
A sense of purpose carries
Somebody down the street.

The sky is tumbling its clouds outside;
It tires of their shapes like a child
And the hands of the clock roll endlessly
Around a segmented heaven.

Yet here
Nothing moves,
Except two huge eyes in their sockets.

Faith

Talking to the dying man,
I justify,
Recycled thoughts in my own mind
That I may mould,
But never give to you unbroken;
For my clay is not supple enough
To give you what you need:

But only a frustrated account
Of a truth which I myself
Cannot grasp:
But try to guide your hands to reach the edges...

The Shiver

The flood of dread that
Follows sinking memory
The sun seeps down below the rooftops,
Spills out its last drops from behind stained clouds,
Sends an absence thundering down the street,
Pulls dismal faces from windows,
Silences trees, and
With a rattling of tattered gateposts,
Chills the fear,
Swells the stride
That pushes on bolder, towards home.

Waiting for the dawn

Wake quickly from a dream of drowning,
And the massive walls are liquid still,
Turbulent shouts and glint-silver
Shapes, turn from the bed and
They're close; TOO CLOSE!
I'm not at the end of this fever sweat.
Line up in a queue and
I'm waiting for the pain and
I'm wishing I were dead and
I wish the night would end.
I'm cold.
And still my huge eyes show the
Fury of my rage,
I'm insane again and grinning,
In the middle of my room
(The picking of the flower and
the grinding of machine). I'm here,
And still I'm waiting for the dawn.

Inside the sphere...

Where shattered colours globe
And bulge
The outside world,
In swirls refracted
And time does not exist.
Everything happens as one instant;
The drop
Silent as prayer
Freefalling pause,
Hangs in its gap
Waiting to shatter this baubell; the
Life: flashed in seconds
Before the crash.

Yawn

Aghast again
And comes the ache
For open, muscled breath-pull:
To shake loose ribs and jaw.
Languish in rounded flood of power
Making its presence known,
A weight swims
Against empty air,
To yell-
Ea-si-ly subsiding,
From stretch
To drop;
    Bewildered!

Figure on the bus

Strange man, stooped
In your faded clothes;
A timid failure, like a child
Abandoned, pathetic to all sorry eyes.

Awkward you are, and I wonder
How you came to be this way;
But my sympathy is shallow -
And quietly I despise you.

Yet at night you listen to the sobbing,
Ease the fears of the lonely,
Answer cries of help; a thankless task
Whilst I am silent:
          I do not know,
            I flinch from knowledge.

And when you lie asleep in bed,
You shall be my judge.

Protest Song

"For Freedom and Justice!"
He announced to his crowd,
Raising a rifle, a sign to fight on.

"Let us be free!"
Was the call that they carried,
Which broke their skulls or left them blind.

"An end to the suffering!"
Was the shout that made widows,
Orphaned the children, lost and afraid.

"For God is with us!"
Was the assurance he gave,
Building an army and crushing the weak.

"For Freedom and Justice!"
Was the call of his youth
But weak and alone his prayer was
"forgive..."

<u>A busfull of faces</u>

In the close formality of the bus
People take their positions.
Crumpled bodies hang in rows,
Cramped by motion and an empty, clattering drone.

Dirty windows mumble a grimy future.
Heads stare vacantly through dead time;
A pessimistic tableau for a stop, which swings attention
And individual passengers, to themselves may return.

Two at a table

"Are these seats taken?"
You shrilled,
I cringed.
The girl, bewildered, could only reply
"No...No they're not"
Then a hint of regret;
The talk had been personal.
The silence was cold
But you didn't notice as you sat
And I followed.
I looked up with apology
But his eyes were turned.

Underplay

We spoke in whispers
As I watched your lips
And cool as liquid-
You knew: I smiled.

This was the danger:
Your voice, a glance,
We touched in a gesture
And both of us guessed.

The Artist

She did not look up
Though the rain beat her window,
Her eyes were steady
On the tip of her brush.

She wasn't aware
Of the shadow-played corners,
Where the room wouldn't keep
Her hugged-in, stilled light.

Her eyes were wide
In breathless fixation
At the revel of colour
That began to emerge:

She did not look up
Until her canvas was satisfied
And when she did, she found-
she was alone.

Siesta

An old woman draped black
Sweeps
Yesterday's thoughts from her balcony floor,
On to the street.

The dust rises,

A tumbled clutter of men
With battered-suitcase faces
Graze on well-oiled stories
And memories, deeply rooted.

A scooter groans in the distance.

Crowds of deserted fishing boats
Eye the tourists for scraps
The sun intruding, strokes the side of my face,
Reminding me of my being:

> "Under the heat of dead time
> Memories mingle with dust
> And aching, settle to sleep".

<u>Sunburst</u>

Bright colours of flowers
Create a thirst
The sun's glint, tilting
Around the side of brittle petals:
Where is the water?..
To lull these leaves in the joy
They show of the life they're aching?

Only the breeze blows temporary comfort,
But that is an illusion;
Leaving sand on the tongue when it stills.

Inside

Sunny days are the worst
For then the room hangs,
Heavy as a carcass
And space between walls is haunted by music,
Practised on some far-off flute;
Unseen, it is abstracted,
It echoes, I don't know where from;
But maddening:
For it creates an unstable background,
Like laughter, blown in through the window,
Or a few loose, fragile words:
So when this curtain sighs its feathered stroke
Across my wall, in the billowing air
It turns my attention
To the sounds of the present,
And I know that I am alone.

Encountered

And just when we thought
The heat would crack,
The car-fumes and dust
Of the city of noise;
The air blanched huge
In the salt of our ache,
The sky ground its throat and
The rain came.

Stinging and bitter
It shattered the road,
Sparking the stone in a
Crumble of cool, sweet
Soothing. The blobbiest
Drops swayed far, with
The easy relief of
Cut grass.

But when the colours of different umbrellas
Scuttled quick down the street
From a rainy applause
Faces grew closer,
Shared shelter and smiles
At the similar, unprepared drench
And you spoke.

You

You wore the mist of morning kettle,
Coffee'd in comfort by early gloom.
Simple rounded objects ooze a smile of satisfaction
And from a swelling yawn of ease I recognised the room.

The chocolate grin of warming liquid
Quivers your cold reflection to my face,
And with the gentle churn of luring river,
The memory of your touch shook into taste.

<u>Questioning</u>

I woke up in a grassy clearing, to the careful stare of some wary deer. The grass was wet around me and yet I was not cold. One of the deer approached, inquisitive, as if to introduce itself to this strange new arrival. The morning mist had just lifted, swiftly from the grass and heavy branches. The sun was bright somewhere but not dazzling, and I was quick and alert on my feet. The scene amused me and I waited for the approaching deer who I knew would have to speak.
"Why are you here?"
The voice sounded like mine, but was too distant to have come from my lips.
"Am I here?"

- I jumped to hear myself speak out loud. My words were brittle against the easy quiet of the wood. The deer also seemed to jump, for, when I spoke it turned its head aside and fixed me with a suspicious eye, then clumped off to join the others.

I wondered what they might be deciding about me and, impatient to find out, I followed, clambering over the longer swathes of grass. The deer nearest to me was alerted by the sound and stared, questioning; trying to work out what I might already know. We stood and eyed each other for several seconds and yet I felt no fear, this creature seemed so honest and open. Suddenly a lack of interest flooded its body and it pulled away from the trance, bending instead to munch at the grass.

As if by this signal the group started to move off, into the trees now the meeting was over. I was eager not to lose them so I followed them as far as a well-worn path. Here they stopped and waited for something, hanging around in the shade or by the grass. I sat on a rock and watched until...

The sound of human voices and trudging startled the group of deer, who fled. Two yellow-anoracked walkers came into view and I recognised one of their voices.
"I don't know!"
I answered to their question, and followed.

Heartland

Slamming the door, I took to the pavement, to the chill of winter evening, where lungs burn cold with harsh gasped air and breath steams white in billows. The darkening gloom of night was pulling over the rooftops, and streetlights drew their lonely glow around them, as guides for the grumbling cars.

My pace was brisk as I passed the houses. Through the windows the brightly-lit lounges shimmered with the blue of burning T.V. screens. I was alone outside. The streets were deserted except for the odd inquisitive car that heaved past, trailing its tired tail-lights and stealing all sound from behind it.

I reached the pathway that led to the forest, its sides flanked by grass and hedges that disappeared into the darkness. A cat darted across my path. I looked up...

Further up the path, and walking the same direction was the back of a figure that looked like a young woman. As I narrowed the gap between us she half turned, not quite daring to look round. I felt the tension; she was afraid of me, this stranger following her along a deserted path - too far to run for help. She quickened her pace, but even though I thought I'd slowed down, the gap between us stayed the same and the crunch of gravel as rhythmically daunting. There was no other path and no other way to go so I quickened upon her until...Just as I could hear her breathing she slowed down and stopped rigid, like a frightened hare. I passed quickly, with tightened steps, knowing her eyes burn into my neck. I took the first track off the path and didn't see her again.

The track was more thickly wooded here and birds were falling out of the sky, to fluster round the clawing trees, chattering a clutter of activity as they did. Around here is hallowed ground. Around here the underground streams seep with life, surprising the rooted limbs of the forest and muscling its massive force through cold earth. This is the place in the hawthorn winter where the wolf, padding low, crushes fear against frost. Here in the dark brimming heart of the forest I held my breath...and listened for the baying for blood.

Intruder

In the tense darkness of the quiet house a strong male figure hugged the shadows, close to the wall. He had been lucky this time, getting in had been easy and almost silent. The deep pile carpet cushioned his careful tread. There was no hurry, he knew that. This was not his first time, and yet he still felt the urge to rush, to bound through the house and get it over with, but that was when you got caught. He was smarter than that. He assured himself that he was not afraid and moved along the hallway to a heavy door that opened out, into a richly furnished dining room, heavy with oil paintings and brittle china ornaments. He ignored them, for he was coldly aware of his task. He crept in and shouldered towards the stairs. There was no light from under the bedroom door, that was good. She would be asleep by now and it would be so much easier. Reaching for the wall next to the stairs he found his hands were thick with sweat. Although he was the only thing awake in the building (there was no dog), the quiet ticking of clocks upstairs was disconcerting, like the gentle pawing of some small animal. He dismissed it and clung to the wall as he edged up the stairs. It was quieter this way, leaning his weight on the wall the stairs wouldn't creak so much.

On the fourth step the squeal of aching wood made him cringe. The noise had been loud and he stopped to listen, to see if it had alerted anyone. There was a mumbling. Someone was awake! His eyes darted quickly for a place to hide but there was nowhere, and he was already too far from the door. He clung to the wall, hardly daring to breath as the clumsy footfalls reached the landing above him. A dazzling light was switched on, hurting his eyes, and now there was another figure at the top of the stairs, silhouetted against the glare of the light "And what time of night do you call this to come home?" called his mother.

First lines of poems | Page